The Essential
Book of
TANTRIC
SEX

The Essential
Book of
TANTRIC
SEX

ANNE JOHNSON

MOON
STONE

First published in Great Britain in 2000 by
Michael O'Mara Books Limited
9 Lion Yard
Tremadoc Road
London SW4 7NQ

ISBN 1-85479-538-4

A CIP catalogue record of this book is available from the British
Library

1 3 5 7 9 10 8 6 4 2

Designed and typeset by Design 23

Printed and bound in Great Britain by
Cox and Wyman Limited, Reading, Berks.

CONTENTS

INTRODUCTION

In today's society, sex is everywhere: undeniable and ubiquitous. It screams at us from every cinema, every TV screen, every newspaper, every magazine, every billboard, and every street corner. That may not be quite to everyone's taste, but we have come to understand nowadays that a satisfying and fulfilling sex life is as important to our physical and spiritual well being as a balanced diet and a good night's sleep.

This realisation may only have dawned on us only recently in the west, but not so in eastern culture. In the east, the giving and receiving of physical pleasure in sexual intercourse has been highly prized for centuries as the supreme act of love. And there is little doubt that we

in the west could learn a thing or two.
To begin with, the attitude to sex in
the west is very different from that in
the east. In western culture, sex is used
as a source of tremendous pleasure or
the means of procreation, but little
more than that. In the east, on the
other hand, it has a third raison d'être:
here sex is also used as a way of
channelling energy towards the
achievement of a higher, or more
spiritual goal. It is seen as a route to
enlightenment – or what the Chinese
call a way of 'provoking the spirit'.

WHAT IS TANTRIC SEX?

But what exactly is tantric sex and what distinguishes it from any other sort of sex? Unfortunately, the origins of tantra have been masked by the mists of time, much of which has passed since the early tantric teachings first began. That said though, tantra is believed to have been sending its students into a state of sexual ecstasy for some 5,000 years.

Tantra is thought to have had its roots in India in Hinduism, from whence it spread to Tibet, China, Nepal, Japan and Southeast Asia. As a result of its widespread distribution throughout the world, tantric symbols can be found in just about every ancient culture, including Stone Age paintings,

Sumerian carvings, Egyptian texts, Hebrew writings, Greek mystical texts, and Arabian love songs.

The heyday of tantra is believed to have been in the 11th and 12th centuries, when it was widely practised in India. Disaster struck in the 13th century, when the Moslem invasion of India brought with it the destruction of tantric manuscripts and the slaughter of many Tantrists. The movement sought safety underground, where it has largely remained ever since those early days, and tantric practice has been largely conducted in hiding.

The word tantra, which was originally an Indian word, means a written text. A tantra is the written equivalent of the spoken version or chant, which is known as a mantra and is often used as the basis for meditation. Similarly, a yantra was a drawing or painting, often geometrical and again used in the process of meditating.

The best-known tantric texts are probably *The Kama Sutra* and *The Ananga Ranga*, which are both ancient Indian erotic manuals, and *The Perfumed Garden*, which is an Arabic treatise on sexual techniques and moral practices written in about 1600 AD.

There are, in fact, several different forms of tantra, depending on the country in which it is practised and the faith that is prevalent there. There are tantric Buddhists, who follow the Asian Buddhist faith; tantric Hindus, who adhere to the Indian system of worship and belief in reincarnation; tantric Taoists (pronounced 'Dowists'), who follow an ancient Chinese philosophy in which the individual aims to find and maintain a maximum level of inner energy, and thus to reach a state of harmony and oneness with the universe; and even tantric agnostics, who hold the view that nothing is known for certain, even the existence of God.

Tantric sex draws on the best of the techniques found in all these ancient cultures. It suggests ways of improving your lovemaking techniques, and it shows you how to alter your sexual focus from the merely physical to the spiritual.

There are two essential, central tenets to tantric sex. One is the overriding importance of the sexual satisfaction of the woman; and the other is the need to control a man's ejaculation.

✺

WESTERN SCEPTICISM

Tantric sex may not, at first glance, appeal to you. Perhaps you're sceptical: what chance is there that tantra, an ancient eastern philosophy of spiritual enlightenment, can effect a change in the love lives of sophisticated western lovers? Can there be any point in examining what the ancient Tantrists, proponents of complex ritualistic practices surrounding the ancient eastern art of lovemaking, had to say?

Admittedly, it probably seems a doubtful proposition. But be patient. It is not hard to extract the essential tantric truths about sexual bliss from their teachings, and to make these easily accessible to the contemporary lover, forever on the lookout for what makes sex good, better and even better.

Surprisingly, this is not mumbo-jumbo. This is a comprehensible and approachable teaching on sexuality, which astonishes by the modern bells that it rings and makes much sense to many.

But whatever your interests in eastern philosophy and in spirituality, the chances are, however, that you might be interested in a way of improving your sex life. Most people are. Many of us go to great lengths to achieve this, and if familiarizing yourself with the teachings of an ancient body of thought dating back some thousands of years offers you a path to sexual bliss, then there seems to be no good reason not to try it.

In the tantric philosophy, sex is about using sexual intimacy as a means of increasing, improving, expanding, exploring and enjoying your spirituality. You and you alone are responsible for your own sexuality and your own spirituality, and the two are linked inextricably. You and only you can change things.

The Tantrists considered sex to be a wholly natural activity – which, of course, it is. Few people would dispute that. But they took this further: they also believed that it is not possible for anything that is natural to be bad, and it is doubtful if everyone will agree with this. The only kind of sex that is bad, according to the Tantrists, is unsatisfactory sex – and that's a very modern way of looking at sexuality, which would not be out of place in any of today's women's magazines.

According to tantric philosophy, all types of sexual experience are allowed. The only justifiable guilt related to sex is if engendered by doing anything that debases it, or if the potential for sexual experience – which is enormous – is wasted. Sex is considered to be an opportunity to learn, and the opportunity to increase

your sexual experience is always good.
If sex gives you pleasure – that too is
good.

Anything that gives you pleasure is
healthy, and good for your physical and
mental wellbeing. As such, sex should
always be an exciting and elevating
experience.

There are no precepts in tantric belief
as to whether sex should only take
place within marriage, or whether sex
outside marriage is wrong. However,
while the question of marriage lines is
not considered to be crucial, the
advantages of sex within a loving and
stable relationship are considered to be
manifold. All the tantric texts make that

perfectly clear. Sex that is not set against a loving background is thought of as second rate.

It is quite wrong to think that tantra advocates sexual abandon. It doesn't – in fact, quite the contrary. Tantra is a surprisingly and deeply moral standpoint. The Tantrists would say that good sex takes time and practice, and that means practice with the same person. You have to become familiar with your lover's needs and likes in order to be a good lover, which is, after all, what we all aim to be. How can you become good at what you are doing if you only do it for the one night? It follows from this belief that Tantrists would be horrified by the idea of a one-night-stand. Sexuality is about sharing your sexual energy, and you can't do this if you're only going for your own sexual gratification. Selfish sex, by definition, is a contradiction in terms and it is definitely not good sex. Love, according to most of the tantric texts, is one of the most powerful energies that a human being can experience. Like sex, love can be channelled to move one's spiritual experience forward.

ENERGY

Much of tantric belief concerns energy, or kundalini to the Indians, ch'i to the Chinese – a way in which it is possible for energy to shift its focus. Tantra regards sexual energy as the most powerful energy there is, and advocates its use as a means of heightening sensitivity, of achieving liberation from the limits of the individual self, and of reaching the highest levels of ecstasy.

Sexual energy can be woken, guided and channelled to increase our wellbeing and our spirituality, culminating in the eventual completion of the tantra, or divine reunion. To the tantric practitioners, sex is not merely about pleasure; it is rather about a deep and fundamental exchange of energy.

Sexual energy is intense, and it is possible to direct it away from the genitals, where it is generally concentrated, to the head and heart.

This makes it possible to have an entirely new climactic experience, where the energy is experienced outside the boundaries of the physical body. Sex is thus elevated to another plane, as the means of achieving the intense joy and inner peace that we all crave and that will revolutionize your life. It is only through a regular experience of great, satisfying sex that you will be able to become a full and rounded person.

Tantric sex may not be something that you have ever considered before. But it is worth investigating. For many people, it has been the means of making what has always been a good experience an even better one. This takes time and practice, but it is worth it. Tantra is not an easy concept for westerners to grasp. Sex, however, as most people would be ready to agree, is a much easier concept to grasp, on a regular and well-practised basis. It is a natural source of intense pleasure, which is experienced by the great majority of people.

But most of us think of that pleasure as a purely physical one, and this is where tantra can teach us a lesson. According to tantric teachings, it is possible to transcend the purely physical and to reach a state of bliss in which time and place have no meaning. Taken to its extreme, it is possible to feel at one with the universe and to achieve a state of cosmic enlightenment.

In the end though, tantric sex will mean very different things to different people. Whether it means cosmic enlightenment for you or better sex, it has much to offer and can make an enormous contribution to our daily lives. Now we have come full circle.

We have returned to the point that a good sex life has a major effect on you and increases your chances of having a long, healthy and happy life. This view offers a totally new take on the art of making love. The tantric approach to the sexual experience can show the path to a longer, happier, better fulfilled and more spiritual way life.

So learn its precepts and follow them. You might even find that tantric sex is one of the best things you have ever done. It might do you untold good. But even if it does nothing quite as life enhancing or as dramatic as that, it should be, at the very least, great fun! So enjoy it!

STARTING
POINTS

Tantric sex, like a lot of new ideas, probably presents you with an entirely new way of thinking and as such, the concept can be a particularly difficult one for westerners to absorb, and even more so to assimilate into their lives. Some people seem to take to it almost instinctively, while for others it presents a much more daunting proposition, involving a massive and troubled leap of faith, which means that the whole process can be a great deal more difficult and take much longer.

Even for those who take to it fairly easily though, tantric sex is not without its difficulties. It involves a great deal more than simply learning something new. It means being prepared to challenge beliefs that you have probably held for years, and to which you unthinkingly hold dear.

There are remarkably few people who do not have a problem breaking with old habits, but this is perfectly normal.

Do not allow yourself to be put off by your doubts – hesitations are only human and show that you don't rush into things without thinking about them, which can be only to the good.

You should be greatly cheered however, by the fact that thousands of people have succeeded in advancing beyond this point, to greater things. So take courage and have confidence in yourself, for you can do it too.

ACCEPTING RESPONSIBILITY

The very first thing that it is necessary for people to do in their search for sexual bliss is to accept that they – and only they – are responsible for their own sexual pleasure. This is an essential first step. It is important to understand that you alone can achieve this. You have to believe it, and you have to believe in yourself. No one else is responsible for your sexual happiness – only you.

This may sound obvious and you may

think that it goes without saying, but not everyone thinks this way. In fact, many people find it surprisingly difficult to accept that their sexual fulfilment is their responsibility. Indeed, many people haven't even thought about it at all, still less taken that all-important first step.

Most people simply make certain assumptions, and the chances are that the assumption they make will be that their sexual happiness is their partner's responsibility. No group is more responsible for this way of thinking than women. If a woman fails to achieve orgasm in her sexual encounters, or if she finds it difficult to do so, she may leap all too quickly to the conclusion that this is her partner's fault. But not so: it is important – indeed vital – for her to realise that it is up to her. This is not only essential, it is also very exciting, because it means that each person's potential to be orgasmic lies within his or her grasp. It is absolutely crucial to think positively.

This is probably the most important thing you can ever do. Never doubt your ability to reach orgasm and thus to achieve sexual bliss. Beyond that initial belief, it will also be necessary to grant yourself both the time, and the necessary space to find out exactly what you should do.

The difficult bit is taking that all-important first step: committing yourself to the firm and uncompromising belief that sexual bliss is indeed within your reach. Having come that far, you will probably find that the rest follows easily.

After that, you must approach the experience of tantric sex not only with a positive attitude, but also with one of delight.

❦

STION OF ENERGY

... more than anything else, a ... on of energy. Sexual energy runs though our bodies, according to ancient tantric belief, rather like a strong electric current. We are born with it, just as we are born with all our other bodily components – our vital organs, for example, or our ability to feel, to breathe, or to speak – and it is there, at our disposal, for us to use wisely and at will. The essence of our sexuality lies in this energy, and finding the true path to sexual bliss is a matter of switching on that all-important current.

Energy runs through the body in a series of complex pathways, or meridians. These are not visible to the eye, but their geography is mapped out in tantric lore.

Sexual energy moves within the human body during sex, and its movement can be both felt and used in a way that is beneficial to us. The energy rises up during the arousal phase of sex and can be channelled in the desired direction. This is an entirely new concept to westerners.

The Hindu tantric texts talk about there being seven energy centres in the human body, which are known as *chakras*, where the body's energy is stored. The *chakras* are represented as lotus flowers, and each petal is supposed to symbolise the blossoming of a particular quality, or area of human life, and is said to control this. Each of the *chakras* has a Hindu god attributed to it, and there are various symbolic animals that are associated with it too, as each is said to be related to certain psychological or spiritual functions.

There are seven principal *chakras* which run up the vertical line of the body from the base of the spine to the top of the head. The seven energy centres are as follows, working from the base upwards.

Muladhara
Also known as the base or root *chakra*,

this is situated at the base of the spine, between the genitals and the anus. It controls our instincts and is a powerful source of desire and is associated with the sensations of life and survival. It is usually shown as a yellow square.

Swadhishthana

Also known as the pelvic *chakra*, this is found at the genitals. It controls our sexuality and is usually shown as a white crescent.

Manipuraka

Also known as the solar plexus or navel *chakra*, this is situated in the centre of the stomach, just below the navel. It controls our personal power and is associated with strength, vitality and ambition. It is usually shown as a red triangle.

Anahata

Also known as the heart *chakra*, this is found in the heart. It controls our love life and is usually shown as a blue hexagon.

Vishuddha

Also known as the throat *chakra*, this is found at the throat. It controls our communication and is associated with speech and creativity. It is usually shown as a white circle.

Ajna

Also known as the brow *chakra* and
sometimes referred to as the third eye,
this is found between the brows. It
controls our intellect and is associated
with intuition, perception and
imagination. It is usually shown as an
upside-down white triangle. The brow
chakra is said to be the home of the God
Shiva. Some proponents of tantric sex
have linked this *chakra* with the feeling
that a person might experience when he
or she arrives at the top of a high
mountain after a laborious climb.

Sahasrara

Also known as the crown *chakra*, this is

situated at the crown of the head, and
is said to connect us with the rest of the
world. It is associated with union and
wisdom. It is not actually a proper
chakra and does not function in quite
the same way as the true *chakras*. The
Goddess Shakti is said to reside here,
and the aim of raising energy from the
base *chakras*, up the spine to the brow
chakras and then on to the crown
chakras, is supposed, according to
ancient tantric lore, to free Shiva so that
he may then be united with Shakti.

This is supposed to enable the union
between the male and the female
principles, which leads to a state of
divine bliss or enlightenment, and for a
person who is lucky enough to have a

well-developed crown *chakras*, sex is a blissful, mystical experience.

Chakras may be either open or closed. There are certain activities, such as yoga, meditation, dance, listening to music and – above all – sex, which will help to hasten the opening of the *chakras*. Such activities are therefore recommended.

This applies, in particular, to tantric sex, which enables you to use your body's sexual energy correctly. The ultimate aim of good sex is to awaken the powerful energy, known as kundalini, which lies dormant at the base of the spine in the base *chakra*.

Kundalini is a Sanskrit word which literally means coiled up, and is usually shown as a sleeping serpent, coiled three and half times with its tail in its mouth. The serpent is capable either of dreadful destruction, or of great healing powers. The idea is that once woken, it will rise up through the *chakras*, and will have a cleansing and de-stressing effect as it rises.

It is also possible to visualise the energy circuit in order to help generate energy. To start with, visualise the base *chakra* and focus your mind on the energy that this generates as it runs up through your seven *chakras*. The idea of tantric sex is that your kundalini energy rises up through your seven *chakras* until it eventually combines with your partner's energy at the tops of both your heads.

THE EXCHANGE OF ENERGY

In good sex, it is important for each partner to find a way of tuning into the energy of the other and, of course, to respond to it accordingly. The idea of exchanging energy during sex is a strange one to westerners, but this sexual energy exchange is very important in tantric belief and occurs on a permanent basis, in the sense that you will carry it with you forever. Thus you will always carry all the energy engendered by your past lovers, and if your sexual experiences are brief, or unsatisfactory, or unhappy, you will carry this negative energy with you and exchange it with your next lover.

Sexual energies are generated and harmonized particularly in some sexual positions, in which partners complete the love circuit by joining together certain parts of their bodies, such as their mouths, their tongues, their hands or even the soles of their feet. This will encourage an emotional closeness between two people and will facilitate a feeling of togetherness between them until, at its extreme, they feel they have reached a complete oneness.

This is another argument for ensuring that all your sexual experiences take place in a loving and stable relationship. Who said that tantra was a licence for sexual abandon, in which love was of no importance? Tantra is actually a highly moral viewpoint, and all the tantric texts hold that sex that is not set against a loving background can only be second rate.

Tantra is a philosophy of oneness, or wholeness, and in order to achieve this, everything is regarded as an opportunity for learning and adding to the gamut of human experience. One of the central tantric beliefs is that tantra embraces opposites, which it regards not as contradictions but rather as complements, which match perfectly to form a whole. Thus male and female are not viewed as opposites, which are set one against the other, but rather as two complementary factors that need each other and that meet in every human being. Everyone, be they male or female, is considered to possess both masculine and feminine characteristics.

According to tantric belief, it is necessary to take this one step further and to encourage the man to recognize, and to become familiar with his female qualities; and similarly the woman to recognize, and to become familiar with her masculine qualities. And in no sphere in life is this more important than in people's sexuality.

To explain exactly what this means and to put it in its sexual context, the male lover is encouraged to explore the soft, compliant, gentle, passive and submissive side of his nature. While the woman, in turn, is encouraged to explore the powerful, dominant, driving, forceful side of hers.

This does not mean that the man has to give up his masculinity entirely, nor that the woman has to give up her femininity entirely. Far from it. It means, rather, that they both have to widen their nature to include the other end of the scale. Successful sexual union is seen as the ultimate union of male and female, and lovers therefore need to be attuned to both their masculine and their feminine qualities.

The two complementary elements of

male and female are represented by the two deities – the God Shiva and the Goddess Shakti, who is his wife. It is from the original union between Shiva and Shakti that the universe is supposed to have sprung. According to Hindu belief, the God Shiva is thought of as a reproductive power and is generally symbolized by a phallus, or *lingam*. The Goddess Shakti, on the other hand, is symbolized by a vagina, or *yoni*. Thus both these deities are heavily laden with rich sexual symbolism and meaning.

⬦

The Taoists had a similar belief. They believed that the world came from the balanced relationship between male and female, which were known in Tao as Yin and Yang. According to the teachings of Tao, the sexual union between man and woman is symbolized by the union between Yin and Yang, or between Heaven and Earth.

Both man and woman possess the qualities of both Yin and Yang, and it is only a question of which is dominant that decides whether an individual is male or female. It is the meeting of Yin and Yang that gives rise to sexual energy, or ching, and this is what results in a life force.

Yin and Yang are represented by a circle, which is divided into two parts. A smoothly curved line between the two separates the Yin, which is black, from the Yang, which is white. In the centre of each half of the Yin-Yang symbol, there is a dot of the opposite colour, which symbolizes the fact that the two are never entirely separate from one another.

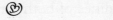

THE BODY AS A TEMPLE

The body is regarded as a temple, the meeting of matter and spirit. The Tantrists therefore had a tremendous respect for their bodies and, in order to prepare the body for the promise of tantric sex, they believed in lavishing a wealth of care and attention on it. They believed in improving fitness levels, which rewards us with healthy and supple bodies.

Being aware of the body and its potential is very important if it is to conspire with us in the attainment of tantric bliss. This is what is required not only for the receipt of physical pleasure, but also for the gift of it to someone else.

❀

YOGA

Yoga is an important preparation in tantric belief. The word yoga is a Hindu one meaning union or joining, which relates to the union of the individual with the deepest level of consciousness. It is a progression of physical postures, or *asanas*, which not only exercise the body by toning the muscles, but also tone the internal organs. Thus yoga tones the entire body, both inside and out.

As a result of this, the highest aim of yoga is to direct the consciousness and the flow of energy inwards, which allows you to experience your body from within. This releases both physical and mental stresses.

Yoga reinforces an awareness of the body, which is one of the most fundamental requirements for great sex.

It is therefore perhaps the best preparation for tantric sex.
It encourages all three of the most important elements of fitness: suppleness, stamina and strength. These are all required as a preparation for all the best lovemaking positions, and in particular those that are especially advanced or complex. Yoga also encourages a peaceful mind, so that it is able to remain clear and focused. Tantric practice requires the mind to be clear and focused at all times.

If yoga is new to you, it would probably be best to join a special yoga group, where you will learn to master the postures. Then, once you are confident about practising these on your own, you should be able to do yoga at home or with a friend.

You may also like to buy a book on yoga – preferably an illustrated one – which will give you detailed instructions as to how to practise each of the postures. It will probably also explain the ways in which each posture is beneficial to particular parts of the body, including particular muscles as well as particular organs and particular bodily functions. Then, as you become more adept, you may still like to attend a regular yoga class, as well as practising at home. An experienced teacher will help ensure that you are doing your postures correctly, and you may also be able to add to your repertoire of postures. It is best to practise yoga on a daily basis, if only for a few minutes each day. The more often you practise these postures, the better you will become at doing them and the easier they will become. You may be surprised, in fact, at how fast you improve, and at the resultant and associated improvements in your suppleness and stamina. Encouraged by this, you will go quickly from strength-to-strength, and yoga will soon become a regular part of your life.

The best times to practise yoga are first thing in the morning or early in the evening, before eating – and preferably at least two hours after eating. Practising first thing in the morning can make all the difference to the day ahead, while early evening practice can help you wind down and relax after a busy day.

Some couples like to practise yoga together, either as part of a class or on their own. This can be fun, and can give you an insight into the respective workings of one another's body. Practising naked can be particularly beneficial, while also giving you a tremendous feeling of togetherness and intimacy.

BREATHING

It is important too, in the practise of
yoga, to pay attention to your breathing
and to make every effort to follow this
correctly. Breathing is something that
we do all day every day and it is all too
often something that we do not do
correctly. Yoga should rectify this and
should also make you aware of your
breathing and your breath control.

There is a branch of yoga, in fact,
known as *pranayama*, in which
breathing is of the utmost importance.

Awareness of your breathing is
important in good sex too, as will be
explained later, and anything that
makes you understand how to breathe

can therefore only be a good thing.

The basic yogic breathing technique is that of the healing breath, and this demonstrates the correct way of breathing.

The best position in which to do this is lying on your back on the floor or on a firm mattress. Place one hand on your stomach as you do this, which will enable you to feel the movement of air in and out of your body as you breathe. Before you start, exhale any stale air out of your lungs, pushing it out through your nose until your lungs are completely empty. Then follow the following breathing exercise.

For this exercise, the breath is divided into three parts: inhalation, retention and exhalation. Breathe in for a count of one, when you will feel your stomach expand; then hold your breath for a count of four; and exhale slowly for a count of two, allowing your stomach to contract again as you empty your lungs.

~

BEING PREPARED

Nowadays, most people are subject to many of the tensions, stresses and strains of modern living, all of which can accumulate until they take their toll on us. There are very few of us who manage to remain totally immune to them and, if we are not careful, we may end up paying a heavy price, both physically and mentally.

We're all so busy these days, and many of us do not have the time to stop and notice the effect that the constant to-ing and fro-ing of our all too overstretched schedules can have on us. We're all too likely to become tired, ratty, nervous and anxious, and one of the first things to suffer can be our sex lives.

So the number one priority if you are to be able to experience the sexual bliss that tantric sex promises is to allow yourself to relax. Take a little time off from your habitually hectic obligations and allow yourself the time to relax, quieten your mind, and find inner peace. This is not a luxury, it's a necessity – and only by doing this are you likely to succeed in opening your inner flow of energy.

Good sex requires both protagonists to be utterly peaceful, quiet and relaxed. It is only when you have succeeded in calming your mind in this way that you will be in the right sort of state to be receptive and to enjoy each moment as your senses awaken. This state of calm receptivity is absolutely vital to good sex.

There are several ways in which it is possible to prepare your mind for the experience of making love. We will investigate these in the pages that follow.

RELAXATION

Effective relaxation is a skill and, just as with any other skill, it has to be learned and practised until it becomes perfect – or as near perfect as possible. That means until it becomes so routine and automatic that it is second nature – rather like brushing the teeth.

Relaxation has many benefits. When you are deeply relaxed, your oxygen consumption – which is equivalent to the rate at which the body burns up energy – will decrease dramatically. It takes some five or six hours of sleep to achieve this low level of oxygen consumption, and everyone knows how recuperative sleep can be. It is not hard to understand therefore, how highly beneficial it may be to rest deeply, and when this can be achieved by only a few minutes of practising a relaxation technique, its benefits are all too obvious. Cardiac output – or the amount of blood that passes through the heart every minute – also falls markedly when you are in a state of deep relaxation, which indicates a substantial reduction in the heart's workload. The heart can never – for obvious reasons – rest completely, but it is clear that working in continuous overdrive can be very harmful, indeed fatal. The heart needs time to recuperate from time to time, and there is no better way of achieving this than by short periods of deep and effective relaxation.

Exactly how you choose to relax is up to you. There are many different ways of relaxing, and different methods suit different people. There are many people who will benefit from taking regular exercise, be it a daily morning swim, a walking regime, or more strenuous exercise such as cycling or jogging. Others find that they can obtain the desired effect from something as simple as listening to music or watching the television. And still others swear by the therapeutic effects of becoming lost in an absorbing book.

The great majority of us, however, require something a little more than that, usually because most of us are a lot more tense than we even realise, and we need to develop some sort of mechanism that will help us relax. None of these is difficult, but that said, they still need to be learned and then practised – only a few minutes spent daily will make all the difference.

There are many possible means of relaxation. Popular methods include deep breathing exercises, deep muscle relaxation, creative visualisation, biofeedback, yoga and meditation.

MEDITATION

Meditation is one of the relaxation methods that is much recommended, in particular, by the tantric masters. It has been practised in the east for centuries and is central, for example, to the yogi's way of life. There are various forms of meditation that have been incorporated into religious experiences and cultures, such as Islamic sufi, Chinese tao, Japanese zen, and so on. Recently, however, the medical profession has recognised that meditation can be an effective form of therapy, which relieves stress and has many well-documented benefits, both psychological and physical. It increases the intake of oxygen, it lowers the heart rate, it reduces the temperature of the body, and it lowers the blood pressure. At the very least, it also allows you time for yourself, which is of tremendous value in this busy, modern world in which we live, buffeted by so many external pressures, demands and obligations.

Meditation enables you to refresh your inner being, which can have a dramatically revitalising effect.
In its common, colloquial sense, the word meditation suggests thinking about a problem, whereas when it is used in the context of relaxation, it means bringing the mind under control in order to free it from all kinds of distracting and intrusive thoughts. This will bring with it a sharp clarity of

mind, which will enable you to savour each and every moment and give you a heightened sense of awareness. This is of benefit in everything you do in your life, not just sex, but it will intensify the relationship between mind and body to such an extent that it will probably be of greatest value in your sexual relations.

Indeed – and this may surprise you – according to tantric teachings, meditation offers one of the most important and supreme sexual techniques. It not only relaxes the mind, leaving it free to be quiet and concentrated, but it also reveals the essential person in you, making it possible for you to get in touch with your inner self.

This allows a more direct and focused communication between two people, which no amount of talking could ever do. And it encourages a healthy flow of energy throughout the human body, which is at the very heart and essence of tantric sex.

MEDITATION TECHNIQUES

The techniques for meditation can be taught, of course, but meditation is not so much about doing something, as about being in a particular state of mind, and that cannot be forced. If you are ready for it, in an open, passive and receptive state of mind that is ready to accept what is going to happen, it will happen spontaneously. This may happen very quickly, or it may take a long time.

However it happens, it's a unique, personal experience, and there is no right or wrong way to do it, and no two people will experience exactly the same thing.

Ideally, meditation should be practised regularly. It will be most beneficial if you practise it for about 10-20 minutes twice a day. Do it in a warm, comfortable place where you can be sure that you won't be disturbed. Take the phone off the hook or put on the answering machine, and if there are other people in the house, explain to them what you are doing and ask them to take care that you are not disturbed.

TRANSCENDENTAL MEDITATION

Meditation involves adopting a comfortable position – usually sitting, though it can equally well be lying or standing – in a quiet room. The classic eastern posture is the yogic lotus, half lotus or cross-legged position, though these are by no means essential.

Another equally acceptable method is to sit on a comfortable upright chair, with your back straight but not stiff, and your body comfortable and still. The tip of your nose should be in line with your navel, and your eyes should be softly shut.

The idea is to concentrate single-mindedly on just one concept. It can be a phrase or word known as a mantra, or an object, such as a flower or a fruit.

This type of meditation is known as transcendental meditation and is based, in part, on Hindu practice. It was introduced into the west by the Maharishi Mahesh Yogi, and received much publicity as a result of its being espoused by the Beatles in the 1970s.

In transcendental meditation, you repeat your mantra to yourself silently, time and time again. A mantra is a completely meaningless word that is unlikely to distract you from what you are doing. Some people use their own name, or the name of a familiar person or thing, which has no significance for them. As you repeat it to yourself, the idea is that your mind will become empty, and you will eventually find it impossible to think of anything else.

You may find that your mind has wandered and that you've started to think about something else, such as what's on television, or what you're having for supper, or something that you forgot to do earlier. If this happens – and it probably will – do not worry – simply start repeating it to yourself again and have another go. Remain passive, and maintain a relaxed attitude towards any distractions of this kind.

Another method is to concentrate in a similar way on an idea, such as a mental picture. Or it can be a question of turning inwards on your own thoughts. Which particular method you decide to choose is, in a sense, immaterial, and it is up to you, depending on your personal intellectual or emotional makeup. Whichever you do, it is an intimate and compelling experience.

BREATHING MEDITATION
Another approach is to bring about a meditative state by a bodily generated rhythm such as breathing. This is probably the simplest method of all. To do this, breathe normally through your nose, while you focus your mind on the sound and feel of your breath as your abdomen rises and falls. Follow the

rhythm of your breath with your thoughts. If you are distracted by other ideas as you do this, don't worry – simply allow them to drift in and out of your head and try to bring your focus back to your breath. Don't force yourself to concentrate – simply let it happen.

Eventually, meditation will become easy and as automatic as falling asleep. When your time is up, take a deep breath, open your eyes, stretch and return to your normal state slowly and gently. The ultimate aim is to discipline your mind to concentrate on one single thing. As concentration becomes deeper, so the whole process of meditation becomes more intense.

WATCHING THE SKY

This is yet another meditative technique. It is, basically, exactly what it says – simply watching the sky.

Don't think about it, don't think about what it looks like – just do it. It doesn't matter whether the sky is blue, dull grey, or gloriously sunny. It is not important. As you stare at it, the idea is to leave everything else in your life behind you until you feel that you are part of the sky. When this occurs, shut your eyes, whereupon you should be able to see in your mind's eye, the picture of the sky that you were looking at before.

Another way of doing this is to look at

a candle. Light it and place it in front of you. Gaze at the candle flame and eventually shut your eyes, you will still be able to see the flame in your mind's eye, just as was described with the sky.

SETTING
THE
SCENE

Rituals are an important part of tantra, and have a lot to do with setting the scene for love. Ritualistic preparation for sex helps it feel really special and important. According to tantric teachings, it is not so much what you do as the time you set aside for it, which shows the importance you attach to love-making.

To the Tantrists, this was a question of honouring your lover in a sacred, almost celebratory way, which they believed allowed you to surrender yourself to the divinity within you. You may not be prepared to go quite that far in your system of beliefs, but it is undoubtedly true that setting the scene can create the right atmosphere and thus the right mood, which plays a useful part in creating bonds of intimacy between two partners.

There are various props that can be used to help set the scene, and different things seem to be right for different people. For some, for example, it is the visual aspect of the room, such as lighting and colours, that plays the most important part, while for others, it is the atmospheric stimuli that count most, such as music and scents.

There are no hard-and-fast rules, but in general men tend to respond better to visual stimuli, and women to atmospheric ones.

The best way forward is probably simply to set aside some time and to devote this to preparing your space, preferably with your partner. Use your imagination and make your preparations as slowly and as carefully as you can. Make sure that you won't be disturbed, and get on with it. Treat it as a shared experience which will benefit both of you, and treat it as a ritual which you can indulge in on every occasion before sex. This takes the sexual experience out of the ordinary, and gives it a special standing. Preparing your loving arena can be an erotic experience in itself, and it can play an important part in kindling the flames of passion, or even rekindling them if the relationship is going through a sticky patch.

LIGHTING

Do you like the lights on or off? Couples frequently disagree as to how much light they enjoy during sex. One may prefer darkness while the other likes to shed some light on the matter, in which case it may be a question of negotiation.

However the mutual preparation for blissful sex is no time to be coy, and unquestionably soft, dim lighting can be seductive. A few lamps set around the room are certainly much more atmospheric than one central ceiling light, which would probably be too stark and rather austere. The light should not be too bright, but should bathe the room in a warm, twinkling glow.

One solution is to opt for candlelight, which – as they say – hides a multitude of sins. It can lend a dramatic, intimate, magical quality to any room, and casts interesting shadows – not only in the room in general, but on naked skin. It can help arouse all the senses, while setting a suitable backdrop against which sexual bliss can occur easily. Always make sure that the candles are placed somewhere safe, where they will not be at risk of setting fire to fabric or flowers, and it is probably better not to put them on the floor, where they could be kicked over easily.

MUSIC

A sexual encounter can be an excellent time for two people to listen to their chosen music together. Listening to a partner's favourite music can be a revealing experience, particularly if your musical tastes differ.

Music can set the mood and can be very atmospheric. It can also affect your energy levels, whether it is quiet, relaxing or stimulating. Tantric sex indicates a need to move away from any inhibition, and music can help you in that direction. Dancing too can have a strong, sexual energy, and tantric teachings encourage a couple to dance, whether together or separately, as a prelude to sex.

SCENT

According to some people, our sense of smell is the most powerful aphrodisiac at our disposal. Accordingly, the use of your favourite fragrance can help create the right atmosphere for sex. A familiar smell can have strong associations and can help reawaken memories of a long-forgotten romantic encounter, while an unfamiliar scent can come as a sudden surprise and can awaken sensual expectations.

Scent the room with a special room fragrancer, or dilute a few drops of a carefully chosen essential oil in water and disperse with a plant sprayer.

THE CLEANSING RITUAL

Bathing or showering together and washing each other before sex can be an enjoyable and important part of foreplay.

Being clean and fresh before making love is always a good idea, allowing for enjoyment of the natural smells of a newly washed body.

But there's much more to washing each other than that. It is also a symbolic act, richly suggestive of the removal of any negative feelings and tensions.

FOOD AND DRINK

Going out to dinner is something in which many couples indulge, and which can play a key part in their relationship. Eating and drinking are highly sensual activities in themselves and they can be a pleasurable prelude to sex. Food and drink can have aphrodisiac qualities and can serve to increase the sensual intensity of any other sensual experience, particularly that of sex.

It is worth adding though, that it is far better not to eat too much. If you end up feeling full and bloated, this will hardly encourage any vigorous sexual activity and it is more likely to make you sleepy. So be cautious, and stick to light meals, eating nutritious, fresh foods that will help with the nourishment and health of both mind and body. Some couples actually enjoy taking food and drink to bed, and most of us agree that breakfast in bed together can be a very sexy thing to indulge in – both before and after sex.

Toast crumbs in the bed and other kinds of mess notwithstanding, eating in bed together can be a lot of fun, and this was something that the Tantrists firmly believed that sex should be!

⇔

DRESSING FOR SEX

The lovers that were depicted in many
Indian pictures were rarely completely
naked, which underlines how erotic a
partially-clothed lover was considered
to be.

The Tantrists believed that it was not
only acceptable to dress provocatively
for your lover, but that it was actually
recommended.

They also approved of ways of
decorating the face and body with
makeup, body paints and jewellery, and
were not averse to the idea of couples
cross-dressing in each other's clothes –
which is a startlingly modern idea.
Anything that makes sex more
enjoyable and takes it out of the

ordinary and humdrum was considered
to be a good idea and to add vitality
and interest to a blissful occupation.

Partially-clothed sex allows for the
friction of body against fabric, which
can be very erotic. Experiment with the
feel of different fabrics – silk sheets, for
example, or fur covers.

Anything that adds interest and
excitement to sex is bound to increase
your enjoyment, and you can be as
daring and as imaginative as you like.

Remember that, according to the
ancient tantric masters, absolutely
nothing is ever forbidden: if it's
pleasurable, it's allowed –

recommended, even – and it's worth giving it a try. So don't hold back, go for it, and enjoy...

BECOMING INTIMATE

Once you have made all your initial preparations for lovemaking, there is nothing to stop you enjoying sexual pleasure. This is what you've been getting ready for.

But there is one other important element that can help your enjoyment of sex.

∾

GETTING IN TOUCH WITH YOUR OWN PLEASURE

Sexual pleasure is an extraordinary thing. Nothing underlines this more forcefully than when you get to know your own body intimately, concentrating in particular on your genital anatomy in a mirror, and come to understand exactly what gives you the most pleasure during the process of sexual arousal and orgasm, while you masturbate.

Masturbation hasn't always received a favourable press in the west, but according to tantric teachings there is no better way of getting to know your own body than through masturbation.

The point is that is impossible to master the art of tantric bliss unless you really know your own body.

The Tantrists believed that masturbation was yet another aspect of a person's sexuality and, as any pleasurable experience is a positive one, it should always be embraced.

Anything pleasurable is allowed, and accordingly, there are many Oriental pictures of people giving themselves pleasure, particularly women.

Nothing enables you to get to know your own body better than masturbation. Understanding what gives you the most pleasure not only allows you to improve the quality of your orgasm but it also enables you to convey this to a partner so that he can do it to you too.

Thus you alone are always the source of your own pleasure. You are the one in control. And showing someone else how to give you the pleasure that you both want and deserve is a very empowering thing to do.

Another plus for masturbation is that it is likely to improve your relationship with your partner. It is through masturbation that you will understand that you are not dependent on him for your own pleasure, and he, in turn, will no longer feel responsible for your pleasure. This will remove a lot of the pressure that he may feel, and puts you both on the same footing.

It is not uncommon for masturbation to engender feelings of guilt in certain people. According to the Tantrists, these feelings are entirely inappropriate.

There is absolutely nothing wrong with giving yourself pleasure and, in any case, the majority of people admit that they do indeed enjoy masturbation.

✧

FEMALE MASTURBATION

The tantric masters suggest that a woman spreads her legs in front of a mirror and looks at herself. She should cover her body with massage oil and stroke her body, moving her hands sensuously over every part of her, in a search for areas that give her extreme pleasure. These are likely to be the genital area, of course, but some of these areas may come as a surprise, such as the inner thighs and the inner arms. The Tantrists believe that the entire body is an erogenous zone and that stimulation of any part of it can cause sexual arousal.

The most attention should be paid to the genital area, which the woman should tease slowly, touching herself gently over the entire area, including the perineum and the anal region. She should experiment with different degrees of pressure, both light and hard, and vary her movements, up and down, from side to side and in circles.

As she brings herself to orgasm, she should keep her tongue touching the roof of her mouth. This is particularly important for Tantrists because it completes the cycle of sexual energy.

As the woman reaches a climax, she should also concentrate on her forehead *chakra*, which pulls the energy upwards – up the spine and through all the *chakras* to the top of the head. This is an ancient tantric practice, which was regarded as an act of great spirituality that was said to bring about a broader consciousness.

MALE MASTURBATION
Similarly, the tantric masters suggest that a man spreads his legs in front of a mirror and looks at himself. He should cover his body with massage oil and stroke his entire body using sensuous movements and searching for areas that give him the most intense pleasure.

Some of these may be obvious but others, such as the nipples, inner thighs and inner arms, may be surprising in the pleasure that they offer. The tantric masters believed that the entire body was an erogenous zone and that stimulation of any part of it could give sexual arousal. The man should now turn his attention to his genitals, including the scrotum, perineum and anus. He should experiment with different kinds of touch, different movements and different degrees of pressure.

As he reaches orgasm, he should keep his tongue touching the roof of his mouth. As with female masturbation, this was regarded as particularly important by the Tantrists because it was believed to complete the cycle of sexual energy. As he reaches his climax, he should also concentrate on his forehead *chakra*, which pulls the energy upwards – up the spine and through all the *chakras* to the top of the head. This is an ancient Tantric practice which was regarded as an act of great spirituality, said to being about a wider consciousness.

MASTURBATING IN FRONT OF A PARTNER

Masturbating in front of a partner is a particularly loving thing to do. It is a way of sharing your most intimate, private sexual behaviour, which establishes a new channel of communication. It is also a means of showing your partner what most pleases you.

Set the scene beforehand, much as you would before making love, and sit opposite one another. Then take it in turns to display your genital area and show how you most like to be touched.

You may, on the other hand, prefer to do this together rather than in turn, in which case neither of you will be on display and the experience will be a mutual, shared one.

MUTUAL MASTURBATION

This is the last stage of sexual exploration, when each partner takes it in turn to give pleasure to the other.

For many couples, this can be the most difficult stage, because it involves a certain abdication of control, but it is worthwhile because it will give you each a better understanding of what gives the other pleasure. It will also create a strong bond of intimacy.

It is a good idea to follow much the same movements and touches that you saw your partner practise on him – or herself. You may not always get everything right first time – few people do – but some degree of trial and error is acceptable. You should each be prepared to help your partner to do the things you like. You can, quite simply, tell one another what you like, or you can make appreciative noises at the appropriate time, or you can adjust your position into something more pleasurable. And in turn, you should always take notice of what your partner indicates that he or she likes best.

Remember that this is a process of communication, and you must be prepared both to indicate and to listen to one another.

MASSAGE

Touch is in all probability our most important sense, and certainly the most telling one in a sexual context. It is something we learn from infancy, and it adds enormously to our ability to communicate and to our sense of security as we grow up. It is sad, though, that as we become older, we tend to lose our use of touch, with the result that we share less and less physical contact with each other.

Touch implies a certain intimacy, which is why some people find it so difficult to use with people with whom they don't have an intimate relationship. Yet touch is very important not only in a sexual context, but also in a much wider sense, because it is such a meaningful way of communicating with people. Always important then, touch becomes even more powerful when it exists in a sexual relationship, where it represents the be all and end all of all intimacy.

Given the importance of touch, massage is a very powerful, meaningful and loving ritual for two people to share. It is not only an excellent method of communicating your feelings about your partner, it is also a useful prelude to lovemaking. It relaxes both the body and the mind, while also encouraging the release of energy, with the result that a person may feel simultaneously both calm and revitalized.

You should always use a sensuous massage oil, which will allow the hands to slide gently and easily over the body.

A wide choice of ready-made massage oils is available from chemists and beauty shops, or you can mix up your own by adding a few drops of your favourite essential oil to a base vegetable oil such as almond or sesame oil.

Each essential oil has a number of properties, so it is worth checking that they are sympathetic to your love-making, as it will be absorbed both by scent and through the pores of the skin and thence into the bloodstream, where it will enhance wellbeing.

The idea is for you each to take it in turns to massage one another. Through the sensual touch of your hands, you will achieve the relaxation of your partner's body, along with a not altogether coincidental arousal of desire.

If you are new to the art of massage, it would probably be a good idea to treat yourself to a really good professional massage, which will give you some idea of what is involved.

Pay attention to the sensations it provokes in you, and then try to create these for your partner by doing it to him or her. Ask your partner to communicate with you as you massage and tell you what feels good, and what is not so good. What we are talking about here is an enjoyable experience, that should also provoke an arousal of desire, so you don't need to take it too seriously or to learn all the ins and outs and the details of every massage movement that you would get in a professional massage. Above all, it should be fun.

Warm the oil a little before you start by standing the bottle of oil in a bowl of warm water. Ensure too, that your hands are warm, because there is nothing relaxing about a freezing cold pair of hands on your body! Start by pouring a little massage oil into one of your hands, and rub your two hands together.

Begin with your partner lying face down on the bed, and spread the oil gently over your partner's back. Massage the upper back, shoulder blades, lower back and buttocks, and on either side of the spine. Then work on each leg and foot in turn. You should always work from the extremities towards the heart, which helps the return of blood to the heart and thus improves a person's cardiovascular health, as well as promoting a general feeling of well-being.

When you have worked on the back, your partner should turn over and you can concentrate on the front of the body, as well as the arms, hands, legs, scalp and face.

~

•

AROUSAL

•

FOREPLAY

By now, you should be ready to make love. Foreplay is the indispensable preliminary to that – indispensable because good sex should never be hurried and because it is only through sensitive and considerate foreplay that you can be quite sure that both partners are absolutely ready for intercourse, both physically and psychologically.

Understandably and rightly, the Tantrists regarded foreplay as a vital part of the ritualistic preparation for sex. It is in itself of great significance in good sex but, as such, foreplay is therefore much more than just a ritual – it is actually an essential requirement in good lovemaking.

Arousal is the first stage in lovemaking, and foreplay is the best, surest and most pleasurable way of ensuring that arousal has taken place.

In a man, it is responsible for making sure that he gets a firm erection, which is of course essential before intercourse can take place.

But it is still more important in a woman, as it is not unusual for a woman to take longer than a man to become aroused. A woman has to be aroused in order for her vaginal secretions to flow sufficiently for her to be ready to accept penetration.

Eastern and western attitudes to foreplay are very different. In the west, it is seen as an adjunct to intercourse and is often rushed because it does not have much more importance attached to it than that. In the east, on the other hand, it is seen as an important and essential part of the overall sexual encounter, which brings with it a great deal of pleasure for both partners, particularly for the woman, though it does not necessarily end in intercourse. This is particularly true in tantric belief.

❦

A WOMAN'S AROUSAL

As far as a woman is concerned, foreplay needs to be a leisurely process, lasting as long as 20 minutes and often a great deal longer. The best way to arouse a woman is with a concentrated and lengthy sequence of movements.

It is best to begin by caressing her head and face. Then slowly move your hands down her neck and shoulders until you get to her breasts. Any firm but gentle movements will work well, including stroking and kneading, as well as kissing and sucking the breasts and nipples. In a particularly orgasmic woman, this can actually be enough to bring her to orgasm.

According to tantric teachings, the whole body is an erogenous zone, not only the genitals, and it is worth remembering this, as you turn your attention to as many other parts of her body as possible. Apply touch not only with your fingers but also with other parts of your body, so you get as much full body contact as possible. This can be highly arousing, so use your imagination and your sensitivity to give her what she wants.

Stroke her abdomen, the inner parts of her arms and thighs, and gradually work your way all over her body until you reach her genitals. Touch her vagina and her clitoris, using both your hands and your mouth and varying the type and pressure of your movements.

Foreplay is not only a matter of arousal. It is also an excellent means of communication between lovers who are attuned to each other's needs, and you should always try to respond to your partner's likes and reactions, and to do what she likes best.

THE KISS

Kissing is particularly important to a woman. Foreplay is not really complete, in fact, unless there has been a lot of deep and sensual kissing. Many women in the west complain that men do not spend enough time kissing, and modern men in the west could learn a lot from the Tantrists.

Tantric teaching recognised the importance of kissing, and considered it to be almost as important a part of lovemaking as intercourse. It is certainly a very intimate activity – all lips, saliva and tongues – which forges a deeply powerful and arousing bond between lovers.

The Tantrists believed that a woman's

upper lip is linked with her palate and her clitoris and that kissing or sucking it can therefore have a profoundly arousing effect on her. A relaxed mouth is, according to tantric teaching, much more sensitive than a tight one, and they recommended kissing with open mouths and open eyes, thus allowing a meaningful exchange of visual contact.

The tongue is capable of both giving and receiving enormous pleasure. It is moist and warm, and it is surprisingly strong and flexible. Use it in any way you like, as the fancy takes you, on your partner's mouth, lips, tongue, teeth, as well as every part of their face and body, from the tip of the nose to the feet. As always, vary the rhythm, speed and pressure of your touch.

According to tantric belief, the exchange of body fluids during lovemaking is very important and, most important of all, is the exchange of saliva. The Tantrists believed that it was necessary to have love, trust and respect for your partner in order to taste their saliva and that once you have done it, you are bound to want to do it again ... and again...

The saliva of a woman who is sexually aroused is known as Jade Fluid and, according to the Tantrists, it is held to be especially advantageous to a man's health and strength. The Tantrists thought that it was important for a woman to touch the roof of her mouth with the tip of her tongue as she approaches orgasm because this completes the cycle of sexual energy.

Then, as she climaxes, she should offer her tongue to her partner so that he can suck her saliva.

A MAN'S AROUSAL
It is considerably easier to arouse a man than a woman, but that is not to say that it should be done without sensitivity and imagination, because – as most men would agree – there is OK foreplay, there is good foreplay, and there is sensational foreplay. Your aim is always to give sensational foreplay.

Full body contact works well for most men, and will arouse both partners in passing. Touch as many parts of his body as possible, and be guided by his reactions – either by what he tells you or by his bodily reaction. Vary the movements and pressure of your touch.

Leave his penis until last, and wait until he is ready to have it touched. Don't worry about being sure – he'll let you know! Men particularly like to have a gentle stimulation of the testicles and the scrotum, and you can use hands, lips and tongue to do this.

ORAL SEX
One of the most compelling ways to

arouse someone, of either sex, is to kiss, lick and suck their genitals. This is clearly a very intimate thing to do. It's also extremely pleasurable for both people, particularly for the partner who is on the receiving end, and the Tantrists approved of it as a highly effective way of sharing sexual energy.

Fellatio, or oral sex on the man, can be done in a variety of different ways, according to how wide the mouth is open and on how wet or dry the mouth is. Vary your oral movements, vary how deep the penis goes in the mouth, and follow what your partner likes best.

Cunnilingus, or oral sex on the woman is often the most effective way of arousing her. According to the Tantrists, the vulva is the most sacred part of a woman's body and a symbol for life itself.

A man should kiss and lick her pubic mound, running his tongue along and between the outer lips of the vagina. You can also put your tongue inside her vagina, making probing movements that can be as deep or shallow, quick or slow, as you like.

The clitoris is the centre of a woman's sexuality, and most women enjoy tongue work on and around it. Sucking the head of the clitoris between your lips can have an almost magical effect, and often results in orgasm – even for those women who generally have trouble reaching a climax.

MUTUAL ORAL SEX

The upside-down or 69 position is an effective way of both partners giving and receiving oral sex at the same time.

Some people prefer to perform oral sex in turn and have trouble finding the right level of concentration when they are doing both at once. For others, however, the 69 position offers a peak of sexual enjoyment.

According to tantric teachings, the perineum is where the base or root *chakra* is located, and is where kundalini energy lies dormant. A recommended tantric practice is to place your tongue on your lover's perineum, when you should actually begin to feel the energy as it uncoils through the *chakras*. This is something you can both do to each other when you are in the 69 position. Try it and see.

∾

PROLONGING
ECSTASY

•

Whichever way you do it, making love is undoubtedly one of life's most pleasurable and most intense experiences. It can never be bad, but there are always ways of making it better, and these require your closest attention.

Don't let this put you off, however. We're not talking about hard work here, merely attention to the feelings of pleasure that you will experience. It's not a question of trying – to make a deliberate effort would risk interfering with your pleasure. It should come naturally, particularly if you're feeling relaxed and maintaining an open attitude to sex. Simply be alert to the pleasures that are to come – this will not only be fun but it will also be well worth it.

MAKING LOVE

Intercourse is the pinnacle of all sexual experiences. There are a great many different ways of doing it, and different people will favour different positions.

Many people don't really have just the one favourite position but like a number of different positions, according to their mood and the circumstances. The important thing is to maintain the variety – a different position for each day of the week, perhaps – and to keep your mind open to a wide range of different and exciting possibilities. If you were always to make love in the same position, and to close your mind to the idea of entertaining the idea of anything different, sex could become boring and predictable.

The tantric attitude to lovemaking is to encourage as much variety as possible, and always to be prepared to try new and different approaches.

Experimentation is always to be recommended, and it is through a constant preparedness to try novelty and variety that you can keep your mind focused on the actual act of sex itself.

According to *The Kama Sutra*, which is one of the oldest and most famous and refreshingly candid works of eroticism ever written, there are in fact very few basic sex positions: these are man-on-top, woman-on-top, and rear entry ones. Anything else is merely regarded as a variation on one of these basic positions. *The Kama Sutra* was in fact compiled around the fourth century AD, but it is actually surprisingly modern in its outlook, and we could all benefit from its teachings.

MAN ON TOP

Man-on-top positions are known as *Uttana-bandha*. These are, for many couples, the preferred ones. This is probably because they allow for full eye contact, which makes them particularly close and intimate.

Maintaining eye contact is considered to be particularly important in tantric sex, because it constitutes such a useful means of intense communication between a couple and enables each partner to know what the other is thinking and feeling. Looking gently and steadily into one another's eyes constitutes a sort of sexual meditation, which lifts the sexual act on to a higher plane. In addition, man-on-top positions allow infinite scope for kissing each other on the mouth, which is greatly favoured by the tantric philosophy of love, with its associated intimacy and intensity.

Man-on-top positions are also favoured in particular by men. This is probably because they give the man full control over all the detailed matters of the intercourse, such as its depth of penetration and its pace.

The most popular man-on-top position is the missionary position, in which the woman lies on her back with her legs wide open. In eastern practice, this is called The Yawning Position.

There are numerous possible variations on the missionary position, according to what the woman chooses to do with her legs. This is the crucial and telling factor. For example, the woman can pull her knees up tightly towards her breasts and rest her feet on his chest, in which case this is called The Position of the Consort of Indra. Or she can wrap her legs around the man's back, in which case this is called The Clasping Position. Another possibility is for both partners to keep their legs straight. One partner presses their legs firmly along the outside of the other's legs in The Pressing Position. Or the man may lie the other way round, with his face turned towards the woman's feet, in which case this is called The Turning Position.

WOMAN ON TOP

Woman-on-top positions are known as *Purushayita-bandha*. As with the man-on-top positions, these also allow for full eye contact, which means they score high marks for intimacy. Eye contact is considered particularly important in tantric sex, because it constitutes such a useful means of intense communication between a couple. And once again, woman-on-top positions also allow plenty of scope for kissing on the mouth, so greatly favoured by the tantric philosophy of love.

When a couple has intercourse this way round, it gives the woman full control over all the detailed matters of the intercourse, such as its depth of penetration and its pace.

The most common and simplest woman-on-top position is when the woman sits astride her partner facing his head, her knees bent on either side of him – this is known as The Pair of Tongs Position. There are many variations on this, the most obvious being when she sits in the opposite direction, facing away from her partner and looking towards his feet. Another variation is when the man sits with his legs crossed and the women sits astride him, with her legs crossed behind his back, in what is a particularly close and tender position.

REAR ENTRY POSITIONS

When a woman adopts a rear entry position, this enables particularly deep penetration and is good if you are in an especially passionate mood. A couple can make love in a rear entry position when they are lying, standing, sitting, or kneeling, which is probably the most passionate position of all. Lying side-by-side in The Spoons Position, with the man lying behind his partner, is an especially peaceful, cuddly position, in which both partners can enjoy a feeling of tremendous togetherness.

REACHING ORGASM

There are two particularly important things during sex that will make it easier for both partners to reach orgasm: one is breathing and the other is pumping the pelvic floor muscles. It is your breath that connects you to your sexual centre – therefore the more deeply you breathe, the closer your connection to your sexual energy.

Breathing deeply enables your senses to intensify, as well as enabling you to feel your sexual responses most intensely, increasing your pleasure and enabling you to realise your orgasmic potential.

Tensing and releasing the pelvic floor muscles in a series of repeated and rhythmic pumping movements as you make love helps intensify feelings of arousal. This is helpful for both men and woman. For men, it helps them delay ejaculation when they are close to orgasm, which is a central tenet in tantric sex (see below), and for women it intensifies blood flow in the genital region and thus increases sensitivity in both the vagina and the clitoris.

THE ORGASM

According to tantric teachings, orgasm is not the end but a beginning, marking a shift in focus from the physical to a deep spiritual experience. It constitutes a potent movement of sexual energy through the *chakras* – from the base *chakra*, at the base of the spine, to the crown *chakra*, at the crown of the head – and thereby releases our spiritual focus.

That's the tantric view of orgasm, but even if you don't subscribe to the entire tantric philosophy, anything that promises better orgasms has to be worth pursuing, and many people – particularly women – have reported that this is indeed the case.

The Tantrists held a substantially different view of the male and the female orgasm. They propounded the belief that female orgasm was of the utmost importance, giving vital life forces, and that female satisfaction was therefore a worthwhile goal. The woman can achieve orgasm time and again, and although she may ejaculate, this does not weaken her.

It may surprise some men to learn that male orgasm, according to the Tantrists, is not synonymous with ejaculation. Men should learn the texts tell us, to control their ejaculations, thus enabling them to make love repeatedly or for prolonged periods of time and to give satisfaction to their female partner over and over again.

Unlike women, men are, in any case, weakened by ejaculation, and should therefore try to avoid it unless they are intending to conceive a baby, which is the only reason for ejaculating.

FEMALE ORGASM

Women are not thought by the Tantrists
to lose energy when they reach orgasm.
Quite the opposite, in fact, as they are
actually thought to gain energy during
sex by absorbing the energy of their
partner, and repeated orgasms are
believed to keep a woman fresh and
young.

This is presumably why masturbation is
regarded as being highly beneficial to
women, and why there are so many
ancient tantric pictures of women
giving themselves pleasure. A lot of
women find it much more difficult than
men to achieve orgasm. This is why it
is good for a woman to masturbate in
front of her partner, so that he can see

exactly what he should do in order to bring her to orgasm.

Women can experience different types of orgasm – the clitoral orgasm and the vaginal orgasm. One is not better than the other, just different, and a woman can learn a lot about her ability to orgasm through masturbation, both on her own and in front of her lover. The Tantrists called the clitoris by several names, such as the lotus bud and the jade pearl. When the clitoris is stroked and caressed, this will bring her to orgasm. The vaginal orgasm, on the other hand, comes about as a result of internal stimulation and it feels very different from the clitoral orgasm. Most women need a much longer period of stimulation in order to achieve a vaginal orgasm.

In addition to the clitoral and the vaginal orgasm, there is also the G-spot orgasm. Many people think that the G-spot is a recent discovery, but in fact the Tantrists were aware of this too, only they called it the hidden jade moon or the heart of the lotus bud. It is located just inside the vulva on the front wall, and is a small area with a slightly tougher feel to it. The man can stimulate the G-spot either with his penis or with his fingers, and a G-spot orgasm causes sharp feelings of the most intense pleasure.

MALE ORGASM

For a man, orgasm is the third stage of his sexual cycle. For the western man, these are the arousal stage, when his penis becomes erect; the plateau phase, when he continues to be excited; orgasm, which is when ejaculation usually happens; and the refractory phase, which is when the penis is flaccid and he needs time to recover before he is able to become aroused again.

For the eastern man, on the other hand, things are different. He does not regard orgasm and ejaculation as synonymous, and he believes that orgasm should be something he can indulge in as frequently as he likes, without the need for a recovery period.

According to tantric belief, semen contains vital life energy. It should therefore be retained and not spent, and the ability to have an orgasm without ejaculating is therefore regarded as a crucial sexual skill.

This may come as a surprise to the western man, who generally believes that ejaculating is a natural and healthy thing to do – if not a tangible proof of his virility and his sexual prowess – and that nothing should be done to interfere with this process. But the ancient Tantrists preached the non-ejaculatory, or 'dry', orgasm, which enables a man to conserve his vitality.

They believed that controlling ejaculation will make a man healthier and stronger, and will, as a result, prolong his life. This will also make his orgasms better because they will become 'whole body' orgasms, which are more intense and more pleasurable.

Lovemaking with orgasms knows no end, and the idea is that men will be able to experience multiple orgasms. The promise is not only better sex but also better and deeper relationships.

§

CONTROLLING EJACULATION

It sounds good – an end to the man who rolls over after his orgasm, energy sapped, and goes to sleep! – but how does he do it? Right from the beginning, the first step a man needs to make is to be prepared to rethink all the ideas with which he was brought up. He needs to abandon all the hype about ejaculating being proof of his manliness and his sexual power. It isn't – it's just an involuntary reflex. He also needs to be prepared to abandon the idea that dominated his youth about ejaculation being some kind of supreme high point – the peak of all sexual experience. In other words, he needs to be prepared to abandon the whole idea of ejaculating. It is not the be all and end all of all sexual experience, and it is in no way essential to sex.

You also have to convince your partner of the wisdom of non-ejaculatory sex, because most women are as guilty as men of elevating ejaculation to some kind of pinnacle of experience. She must not regard your ejaculation as proof of the strength of your feelings, or even of your love for her. Ejaculation is very far from being a magical experience, or any kind of ritualistic proof of what a man feels in his heart.

This is mystical claptrap, and your partner must co-operate in this. She must understand, and sympathise with, your aims.

Having done that, you're halfway there. What you now need to do is to redirect your sexual energy and to concentrate on retaining it within your own body and from there to your partner. This is a question of much more than merely preventing ejaculation. It's rather a question of understanding how your body works – your sexual rhythms, what makes you more or less likely to ejaculate, what sexual positions are more or less conducive to ejaculation, and when ejaculation is near, imminent even, and inevitable.

THE NUTS AND BOLTS

There are several things that you can do in an attempt to control your ejaculation. For some men, one of these methods may prove to be enough. For others, it is better to find your own combination of methods, until you find a system that works. Don't expect success first time, and don't be put off by the occasional failure. This takes time, patience and practice, but if you believe in your ability to do it, you are more likely to succeed. As with just about any skill, you will get better at it as you practise – so don't be impatient, you'll get there in the end. Sex is a learning experience, and the rewards on offer are to be learned and enjoyed.

Westerners tend to indulge in sex only when passions overcome us, but according to tantric teachings it is better to set aside a special time and place when both partners can practise what they have learned together. With concentration and practice, ejaculation control will become much easier to cope with.

One thing that many men find helpful is to concentrate on keeping very still. Summon up all your concentration, and relax every muscle in the genital region, including the anal muscles.

Another helpful move is to press your tongue against the roof of your mouth, about 1cm/½ inch behind your front teeth. You will probably find that this has the extraordinary and surprising effect of anchoring you, which helps redirect your sexual energy back down the front of your body to the base *chakra*, at the base of the spine, whence it came. This should also have the effect of delaying, or stopping, ejaculation.

Take a series of deep, regular breaths. This will have the effect of slowing down your heart rate, indeed slowing you down generally and will put a halt to the urgent need to ejaculate.

Withdraw your penis a little from your partner's vagina. This does not have to interrupt or spoil intercourse because then, when your need to ejaculate has subsided, you should be able to recommence thrusting and penetrating deeper again.

If the latter method fails to work, you may try taking your penis out of your partner's vagina altogether. Wait until you feel you are able to start proceedings again without ejaculating.

Press the index and middle finger of one hand quite hard against your perineum, the area halfway between your scrotum and your anus. This will have the effect of keeping semen in the prostate, where it will be reabsorbed by the body in the bloodstream. If you prefer, and as you get better at it, you might ask your partner to do this. This will make it a mutual enterprise, which is always a good thing to do.

Place the thumb on the underside of the penis, with the index and middle fingers on the ridge of the glans on the upper side, and squeeze for 10-15 seconds or so, until you have lost the urge to ejaculate. You will probably also lose your erection, but you will be surprised at how easy it is to get another one. You partner can use this 'squeeze' technique if you prefer, and again, it is surprising how pleasant it can be to make a joint attempt at controlling your need to ejaculate.

❧

THE WHOLE BODY ORGASM

Once you have mastered the art of controlling ejaculation, you should be able to use a combination of arousal, relaxation and deep breathing, which will allow you to have a whole body orgasm. This is just what it says, a climax that affects the entire body rather than a localised genital orgasm. It is reported as feeling much more subtle than a genital orgasm, and is less of a quick thrill, or a momentary burst of excitement, than a continuous, on-going surge of pleasure.

THE AFTERGLOW

After sex, there is the afterglow. This is a time of friendship, warmth and closeness. It is not a time for rolling over and falling asleep. This is a special time, and it is important not to rush it. It is a time for lovers to enjoy each other, while they are feeling completely relaxed, content and satisfied.